The Pawnee Indians:

Proud Yet Peaceful People of the Stars

In60Learning

Sign up for the LearningList
to receive

eBooks and Audiobooks

at
www.in60Learning.com
Smarter in 60 minutes.

CONTENTS

PAWNEE INDIANS: FARMERS OF THE PLAINS

From perhaps as early as the 1200s, the Pawnee Indians made their home in settlements in the Platte and Loup River valleys in what is now known as Nebraska. Their ancestors settled in that area from the Ohio River Valley. They eventually formed four distinct groups, or bands: The Chaui, or Grand; The Skidi, or Wolf Pawnee; The Kitkehaki, or Republic Pawnee; and The Pitahauerat, or Tapage Pawnee. Although each band was essentially autonomous, the Chaui was considered the head group. The Pawnees were a proud, strong, and peace-loving people who believed that they were the greatest people on Earth. In fact, they referred to themselves as Chahiksichahiks, or "men of men."

What set the Pawnees apart from other Plains Indian tribes is that they lived in permanent settlements with earthen lodges and relied on agriculture to supplement their hunting. They were also unique among their contemporaries in that they practiced human sacrifice as a way to appease the gods and ensure an abundant crop. Additionally, their spirituality was intrinsically tied to the stars, to which they referenced when sowing crops and establishing villages.

Although the Pawnee likely encountered Spanish explorers as early as the mid-1500s, regular encounters with European settlers really began in the 1700s. The Louisiana Purchase in 1803 meant that Pawnee land was now owned by the United States and the Pawnees wrestled with the concept of land ownership, which was a foreign idea to them. After deeding their native land to the U.S government, under the conditions of several treaties spanning from 1833 to 1876, the talk of resettling the Pawnee Indians on land that was designated Indian Territory in Oklahoma began in earnest. The issue of resettlement caused a deep divide among the four bands of the Pawnee, but they united together to seek the protection of the United States government following a war with the Dakota Indians in 1873. The removal of the Pawnees from their tribal homeland in Nebraska started the following year and ended in 1876. The Pawnees struggled to maintain their traditional way of life while living on the reservation and there were too many changes that occurred for them to keep their culture entirely intact. Today's Pawnee Indians celebrate their culture and heritage with biannual gatherings, or Powwows.

1 LIFE IN THE PAWNEE VILLAGE

"You must not hurt anybody or do harm to anyone. You must not fight.
Do right always. It will give you satisfaction in life."
~Wovoka, aka Jack Wilson

The Pawnee people were organized into villages. Although the numbers vary greatly, on average, each village was made up of between 40 to 200 lodges that each housed up to 80 people. Therefore, village populations ranged from 800 to 3,500 people. Presiding over the affairs of the village was a band of four chiefs, a head chief and three lesser chiefs. The position of chief was a powerful one as it was the voice of authority for the village. New chiefs often earned their title through family succession, but sometimes the title of chief was bestowed upon a warrior based on his successes and achievements in battle. Assisting the band of chiefs were younger boys who served as pages or criers. They helped the chiefs with basic, day-to-day duties and shared announcements and proclamations to the people of the village.

In the social order of the Pawnee community, the chiefs were at the top of the pyramid. Just below the chiefs in the social order were the warriors and below them were the spiritual leaders and the medicine men. Further down the line were the common village people who lacked power and influence. Toward the bottom of the social hierarchy was a group of people who had violated some tribal law and was living as a semi-outcast just outside the village. The very bottom of the pyramid was slaves, mostly non-Pawnee Native Americans who were captured in battle and enslaved. In addition to the stringent hierarchy, there were community organizations comprised of men from the village that oversaw different aspects of village life. Each of the four chiefs had four warriors that enforced his orders. The band of medicine men formed separate groups.

The role of women in the social order was underplayed, as men handled what was deemed the most important functions in the society – hunting, fighting, and praying. Yet women in Pawnee culture were entrusted with vital roles. The chief's wife, for example, was solely responsible for the care and maintenance of the village's sacred bundle. The sacred bundle was the most sacred item in the village and contained objects of great spiritual significant to the tribe members. The priests, or spiritual leaders of the community, used the sacred bundle for rituals and ceremonies. Although it was "owned" by the head chief, it was an important symbol of the pride and unity of the whole village. It speaks volumes about the trust and responsibility of women in the Pawnee society that the chief's wife was the caretaker of such a valued and powerful totem.

The role of the spiritual leaders in the Pawnee village was to serve as mediators between the people of Earth and the gods of the heavens. Specific priests were tasked with maintaining the tribe's good graces with the deities that controlled such things as the success of a hunt, weather, fertility, victory in battle, and yield of the harvest. By performing complex rituals and ceremonies at altars devoted to the Morning Star and the Evening Star, these priests would request favor from the gods.

Medicine men in the Pawnee village were more practiced in spiritual healing and prayer than they were in traditional medicine. The deities that oversaw health and well-being of the village members were animals, each with a unique curative capacity. Earthly animals, embodied by these deities, could bring illness to a person. The Pawnee believed that the animals had an animal lodge, possibly located along the banks of a river or even under the water itself, where they all congregated. Much like the Pawnee medicine men working in their doctors' lodge, the different species of animals would unite to bring their individual powers together to aid a person in need. One or more of these animals would appear to a person who was sick or injured and bring with them healing vibes. The animals could also mesmerize a person and put him in a trance-like state. Pawnee men suffering from a malady would lie down near a river bank and go to sleep. In his sleep, an animal deity would mesmerize him, take him into the animals' underwater lodge, and gift him with healing wisdom.

Although the Pawnee were fierce fighters, they valued peace within their own communities. Societal rules and laws were in place to control violence among the people of the village. A small band of Pawnee men served as police officers in the village and they were supervised by the head chief. Their task was to stop in-fighting and prevent violence, ensuring a peaceful existence. A person caught breaking a tribal rule was banished to the outskirts of the village until he proved himself a worthy member of the community. During the annual buffalo hunts, the police squad made sure that certain disruptive or over-eager hunters remained at camp so they could not bother the herds of buffalo and disrupt the hunt.

Family lineage in the Pawnee tradition was matriarchal, meaning it followed the mother's family tree. Because of this, when a couple married, they would often move into the bride's parents' lodge. The mother's brother arranged for the marriages of his nieces to suitable mates, almost always staying within the family's social class. Polygamy was common in the Pawnee culture and was strictly sororal, meaning sisters were wed to the same husband. Marriages between relatives, including first cousins, were forbidden. Youngsters were raised by grandparents or other village elders who instructed them on village customs and societal norms, while enforcing strict discipline. Children in the Pawnee village enjoyed sexual freedom until puberty, when they were not allowed to interact with members of the opposite sex until they married. But they recognized the sexual urges and desires of young men and encouraged them to gain sexual experience before marriage. The young man's mother's brother's wife could be used as a sexual partner and teacher for the young man from the time he reached puberty until he married.

Social order remained important into the afterlife. People of higher social class, people who died bravely in battle, or people who died well into old age received special after-death treatment. They were anointed with sacred red paint and dressed in the finest clothes before being wrapped in a buffalo hide and buried. Pawnee who died bravely, heroically, or honorably became stars in the afterlife. However, if a person died in a cowardly manner or succumbed to disease, their souls would reside in the Village of Spirits, vaguely located "to the south."

2 HUNTING AND FARMING IN THE PAWNEE VILLAGE

"You ask me to plow the ground. Shall I take a knife and tear my mother's breast?"
~Wovoka, aka Jack Wilson

Most of the Native American tribes of the Plains were nomadic in nature, moving their settlements from place to place to follow the seasonal migration of the animals they hunted. This was not so for the Pawnee. They put down roots…in their permanently-established villages and their fields of crops.

Prior to 1833, there were four main clusters of villages in the Pawnee nation. Each village contained between 10 to 15 lodges, each housing about 30 to 50 people. The lodges were oval-shaped and large, constructed of solid wooden posts and covered with willow boughs, dirt, and grass. On average, these lodges were as tall as 15 feet in height and about 40 feet in diameter. Although the lodges were permanent structures, they weren't permanently occupied. During the warm summer months, most of the people chose to sleep outside, under temporary lean-tos. Twice a year, when the Pawnee hunters left the villages to hunt bison, they used portable tepees of buffalo hide for shelter. Many Pawnee villages were encircled by a low wall, about three feet high, made of earth and sod. This served as a way for the warriors to defend the village from invaders.

The villages were arranged based on star constellations and served as a permanent testament to important star clusters. On opposite sides of the village were altars dedicated to the Morning Star and to the Evening Star. These were important shrines, and the people of the village frequently visited them. The four corner posts of the lodge houses pointed to the northeast, northwest, southeast, and southwest because the Pawnee people believed that the star gods lived at these compass points and, from there, they held up the sky. The doors of the lodge could directly face the east and the rising sun.

Surrounding the village would be farm fields. The Pawnee were experienced farmers and took advantage of the rich, prairie soil to grow their crops. Although they cultivated sunflower seeds, prairie turnips, melons, pumpkins, and spinach, the mainstay of Pawnee agriculture was the Three Sisters – maize, beans, and squash.

Several other Native American tribes, along with the Pawnee, also grew maize, beans, and squash in a companion growing situation. To conserve land and enhance the harvest, the three plants were grown together in a mound. The maize, or corn, was planted first, and when the young sprouts were about half a foot tall, the winter squash and climbing beans were planted next to it. These three crops together form an ideal companion planting. The beans twine around the corn stalk and add nitrogen to the soil. The squash vines stay low to the ground and spread quickly. Their large leaves block out the sun and prevent weed growth. The leaves also help the soil retain moisture. Botanists estimate that it took more than 5,000 years of farming for Native Americans to develop this system of companion planting. They have also noted that the three plants were not domesticated all at the same time. Squash was the first to be cultivated by the Native Americans, followed by corn, which they call maize. The last of the three to be domesticated was beans.

The Pawnee people, along with other Native American groups, considered the Three Sisters plants to be gifts to humans from the gods because they were such important food items. All three vegetables – beans, squash, and corn – are high in essential fatty acids and amino acids. They contain complex carbohydrates that fuel the body for strenuous work. Additionally, all three of these vegetables can be stored for long periods of time or dried for storage over the barren winter months. A bountiful harvest of the Three Sisters would ensure the survival of the tribe, even in the harshest of winters.

So vital was the Three Sisters to the way of life for Plains Native Americans that the three vegetables found their way into folklore. In one such tale, there was a family with three daughters. The three sisters were all unique and very independent. The oldest sister stood tall and straight with silky hair. The middle sister was short and broad and muscular. The third sister was average height and adventurous in spirit. Much to their parents' displeasure, the three sisters fought with each other and their arguing kept them from their work in the garden. The parents fretted that their crops would fail and they would starve over the winter months. They asked the gods to help them. When they looked out into their garden, they saw that the oldest girl had been transformed into a tall stalk of maize, the middle sister had turned into the low, hardy squash, and the youngest sister became a climbing bean vine. At last, the three sisters learned to work together to help provide for their family and their village.

Of course, these vegetables were supplemented with meat from hunting. The Pawnee hunters used their bows and arrows to hunt and kill the small and medium sized game animals of the grasslands; deer, elk, turkey, grouse, rabbits, prairie chickens, and even bears. When the Spanish explorers introduced horses to the Pawnee and other Plains Indians, the Pawnee began buffalo hunting in earnest. Seasonal buffalo hunts yielded plenty of meat that the Pawnee dried into pemmican. Pemmican was made from dried meat that had been pounded into shreds, mixed with melted animal fat, and left to solidify into cakes. Nutritious and packed with protein, pemmican could also sustain the people of the Pawnee village when hunting was scarce.

The fact that maize, beans, and squash are collectively known as the Three Sisters and not the three brothers may be indicative of the division of labor among genders in the Pawnee culture. Pawnee women most often tended to the gardens while the Pawnee men hunted. The spiritual leaders of the village, who were all males, participated in planting and harvesting the crops by conducting ritual prayers and beseeching the gods to provide a plentiful yield at harvest time. The women, however, played an important role in food preservation. The task fell to them to dry the vegetables and meats and prepare the foods for winter storage.

Cooking meals was also the responsibility of the female members of the village. Several families often lived together in a large lodge house in the village and meals were shared experiences. When ceremonies were scheduled, the Pawnee women worked alongside each other to prepare food for the feasting. One such cerebration was a send-off to the summer hunting parties.

In early summer, the Pawnee hunters and many of the other village members left the permanent settlements and lived, temporarily, like nomads while hunting. During this time, they utilized portable tepees that could be moved easily from place to place. The hunters brought their kills back to the temporary camps and the women skinned and processed the animals. The hides were tanned to be used as robes, clothing, or blankets, or to construct new lodge houses. Antlers and bones were worked into tools, such as hoes, awls, and scrapers. As summer neared its end, the hunting party would load up their spoils and return to the village. This often coincided with the beginning of harvest time.

Because many Pawnee villages were located along the Platte River or other large rivers, the Pawnees looked to the waterways for food as well.

Sturgeon was plentiful in the swift waters so the Pawnee people learned to catch the fish and dried this meat in the same way they dried deer and buffalo meat. They also found crayfish and mussels along the banks of the rivers.

3 SPIRITUALITY IN THE PAWNEE CULTURE

"In the beginning of all things, wisdom and knowledge were with the animals, for Tirawa, the One Above, did not speak directly to man. He sent certain animals to tell men that he showed himself through the beasts, and that from them, and from the stars and the sun and moon should man learn."
~ Eagle Chief Letakos-Lesa, Pawnee Chief

The Pawnee religion was so very ingrained in the everyday lives of the Pawnee people that European missionaries could not easily sway them to Christianity, no matter how hard they tried. As a whole, the Pawnee Indians did not fully convert to Christianity until the late 1800s.

Like most Native American tribes, the Pawnee people were deeply spiritual. Their polytheistic, primary belief system stressed the need to maintain a harmonious balance between nature and the gods. The main deity, Tirawa, is the master over all of the sky and the Earth but he cannot be seen by humans nor can he interact with them. Next in the spiritual hierarchy are the Red Morning Star and the Evening Star. The Morning Star, a masculine god, reigned over fire and light and dwelled in the eastern sky. The feminine Evening Star called the western sky her home and she ruled over darkness and fertility.

Situated below Tirawa and the Morning Star and Evening Star were a series of lesser gods who lived in the great circle of the sky. The first of these lesser deities were the winds. The four winds represent the intercardinal directions of north-east, north-west, south-east, and south-west. In the Pawnee creationist myths, the winds were the first gods to approach the newly-created humans and serve as their protectors. The four winds are ever-present and stand at the ready to help mankind when needed. They are also sentinels who guard the path that leads from the great circle of the sky to Earth. It is this pathway that the other gods use when they descend to Earth to help man.

Other lesser gods of the Pawnee religion include Mother Earth, the Sun, Water, and Fire. Mother Earth is a sacred deity because she provides the very foundation for Pawnee life. The Pawnee people build their lodges on her and lay down on her to sleep. She provides them with food, particularly maize, the food plant gifted to humans by the gods. The Sun provided warmth and light and represented power and might. Without the Sun's blessing, the Pawnee people knew the crops would not grow and the people would starve. Water was also necessary for life and the Pawnee people were grateful for the rains that fell from the sky and the great rivers that flowed through their lands. The Pawnees believed that the gods sent both of these to the humans. Fire was an answered prayer for the Pawnee Indians and was given to them through the god Toharu. Toharu is the vegetation that covers the Earth, including the grasses and trees. Toharu gave man the ability to start fire by rubbing two sticks together.

The Pawnee Indians found spiritual links in nature and wove these beliefs into their culture. For example, they regarded the eagle as the great chief of the daytime and the owl as the great chief of the nighttime. The chief of the water was the duck, and the woodpecker was the chief of the trees. The hills were given to mankind as a gift from the creator Tirawa. The hills allowed man to ascend closer to the sky and the gods during special prayers, but also provided a vantage point for scouting the enemies.

Typical of the Plains Indians, the Pawnee people utilized sweat lodges. These long, low structures were designed to keep the heat from fires inside the building. The people inside endured a purification ceremony led by a priest or religious elder. Intended for deep prayer and spiritual healing, the purification was thought to be achieved through excessive sweating. The Pawnee Vision Quest was another Pawnee ceremony that marked a boy's passage into manhood. Central to religious celebrations was the sacred pipe, also known as a Calumet. The Calumet was passed around to the attendants who all smoked the tobacco. The Vision Quest, also directed by a priest or elder, involved prayer and fasting and isolating the young man in the wilderness alone. There he could commune with the animals that were, according to belief, messengers from the gods, including Tirawa.

Presiding over the religious and spiritual affairs of the tribe was a group of wise men. These men were bestowed their position of power by familial succession, fathers handing down the authority to their sons. This group of spiritual leaders was the go-between linking the other tribe members and Tirawa. In addition to overseeing the everyday religious matters of the tribe, they also organized and guided the various ceremonies that were needed to appease the gods.

Sacred bundles were an integral part of the Pawnee spirituality. Each Pawnee village had its own sacred bundle which was comprised of items with special significance and meaning. The sacred bundle protected the village from evil and ensured prosperity.

Human sacrifice was part of the Pawnee rituals. This practice was unique to the Pawnees, as other Plains Indians did not utilize this custom. Called the "Morning Star ceremony," the event was conducted as a show of devotion to the feminine deity, the Morning Star, and a young female was the sacrificial offering. Although most of the Pawnee rituals were closely tied to specific times of the year, as depicted by their star charts, the Morning Star ceremony was not. The ceremony was planned when a Pawnee warrior dreamt of the Morning Star, then viewed it in the sky when he awoke at dawn. This was a sign that the warrior needed to initiate the ritual that would give guaranteed achievement in battle and a hardy virility.

The first step in the process was for the warrior to raid a nearby village to abduct a young maiden to be sacrificed. For days leading up to the ceremony, the prisoner was housed with her captor who fed her the finest food available using dishes and utensils from the village's sacred bundle. The entire village was involved in the Morning Star celebration. Feasting, dancing, singing and drumming took place. The spiritual leaders of the village then dressed the kidnapped girl in special clothing and painted her face with red coloring. Early one morning, as the Morning Star watched, she was taken to a platform constructed using symbolic kinds of wood. The victim was ceremoniously shot with a sacred bow and arrow, after which, her chest was cut open. Drops of her blood were drizzled onto buffalo meat that was then cooked and served to the whole village. Before the feasting could begin, however, every member of the village -- from young to old -- stabbed arrows into the victim's body. The sacrificial maiden, according to Pawnee beliefs, was then released into the heavens where she became a new star.

The practice of human sacrifice by the Pawnee people gained national attention when a Pawnee chief named Petalesharo was featured in newspapers around the country for rescuing a young Comanche girl who was abducted for sacrifice in 1817. Both Petalesharo and his father, Knife Chief, had openly expressed their disdain for the practice, but the tribes people clung to the belief that the sacrifice was necessary for a bountiful harvest and successful hunt. When the Comanche girl was led to the scaffold and the archer prepared to kill her, Petalesharo stepped in and announced that he and the chief condemned the sacrifice. He gave the girl a horse, food, and water and sent her back to her tribal village.

The story of Petalesharo's actions spread to surrounding areas and soon Christian missionaries heard the tale. A highly-sensationalized account of the rescue was published on November 22, 1821, in *The Washington Daily National Intelligencer*. Shortly afterwards, another newspaper, the *New York Commercial Advertiser*, printed a poem called "The Pawnee Brave" which became wildly popular.

Because of his growing popularity, Petalasharo was invited to Washington D.C. by Thomas L. McKenney, the Superintendent of Indian Affairs, and Benjamin O'Fallon, Indian Agent. While using the auspice of showcasing the Native American culture to lawmakers in the nation's capitol and commending the bravery of Indians like Petalasharo, the government had ulterior motives for inviting a delegation of Native Americans to Washington. They hoped to tout the power and might of the white man in hopes of intimidating the Native Americans so they would cease attacks on settlers and prevent possible attacks on the government itself. In addition, the Native Americans demonstrated ceremonial dances, met President James Monroe, and had their portraits painted by Charles Bird King. Petalasharo also met with James Fenimore Cooper during his visit to the east. This meeting inspired Cooper to write a novel, "The Prairie."

A spiritual movement called the "Ghost Dance" began in 1870 as a unifying effort to increase awareness about the traditional Indian heritage in the wake of displacement and resettlement by the United States government. The Ghost Dance movement gained momentum after a shaman of a Paiute Indian tribe named Wovoka, or Jack Wilson, announced that he saw a vision during the solar eclipse of 1889. His vision depicted the evils of the white man and an apocalyptic destruction of the land, after which a reborn Earth would again be solely inhabited by the Native Americans. The Ghost Dance involved frequent ceremonies with dancing that lasted for five consecutive days. Although the Ghost Dance religion was viewed as instilling pride and hope in the Native Americans, many others feared that it was a prelude to an Indian uprising. The Bureau of Indian Affairs eventually banned the Ghost Dance.

4 STAR WATCHERS

"The Skidi saw a sky of glorious beauty…their Spirit Path, the Milky Way,
loomed overhead in brilliant splendor."
~Von Del Chamberlain, author of *When Stars Came Down to Earth*

Very few trees grew on the Nebraskan plains where the Pawnee Indians
made their homes. Most of the trees grew along the banks of the Platte,
Republican, and Loup rivers, giving the Pawnee people an unobstructed
view of the night sky. The Pawnees observed the sky and studied and
documented the movement of the stars. They were the preeminent sky
watchers of the Plains and they developed one of the most complex and
sophisticated astronomy-based belief systems of all the native, North
American Indian cultures.

The Pawnee placed great emphasis on the position of celestial bodies
and it became ingrained into their everyday life. Star symbols and motifs
adorned their ceremonial robes and the walls of their tepees and lodges.
They created star charts, often on buckskin, that documented the placement
of the stars.

The Pawnee people believed that their ancestors were born in the stars.
Tirawa, the principle god of Pawnee mythology, controlled the movement
of the stars and created the Path of the Departed Spirits, otherwise known
as the Milky Way. In their creationism myth, a daughter was born to the
male Red Morning Star, who lived east of the Path, and the female Evening
Star, who lived west of the Path, but not until after some pursuing on the
part of the Red Morning Star and some coy, flirtatious stalling on the part
of the Evening Star. When the Red Morning Star made his romantic
advances on the Evening Star, she dodged his efforts and placed ten

obstacles in his way. She did this not to be a tease, but because the Earth was not yet ready for human inhabitants. When their daughter eventually was born, she was laid on a cloud and descended to Earth to live in a celestial garden. In this garden, many plants grew, watered by the Red Morning Star. One important plant was the food plant maize, which was given to the daughter by her mother, the Evening Star, as a gift to the Earth.

The Moon and the Sun conceived a son who joined the Red Morning Star and the Evening Star's daughter in the celestial garden. They married, and the daughter was the one who gave birth to the human race. The human race was then, according the Pawnee belief, the descendent of four significant, celestial bodies; the morning star, the evening star, the sun, and the moon.

The stars remained vital to the Pawnee way of life. The stars served as a way of marking time, they looked to the stars to tell them when to plant and harvest their crops, and when to host significant ceremonies and rituals. The detailed observations of the stars helped them create a star calendar that was sophisticated and accurate. Their star charts recorded not only the movement of stars, but showed that the Pawnee astronomers were knowledgeable about comets, meteorites, and five of the planets in the solar system.

To make their observations of the night sky, the Pawnee people constructed their lodge houses to align with the eastern sky. The four corner posts of the lodges all coordinated with the cardinal directions. In fact, the orientation of the Pawnee observation lodges was so precisely aligned with the east-west configuration, that the first rays of sunlight on the morning of the vernal equinox would fall on the altar. The lodge's smoke hole lined up with the Pleiades star constellation, and the Pawnee sky watchers used this constellation to track the time of night.

The Pleiades constellation was of particular importance to the Pawnee people, as was the Corona Borealis. While many cultures centered myths around the Pleiades and refer to them as the "Seven Sisters," the Pawnees consider this star cluster to be the "Seven Brothers." In the Pawnee culture, November is nicknamed "the time of the Pleiades" because this is the time of year that the constellation can be seen in the sky from sundown to sun up. The constellation known as Corona Borealis was called the "Circle of Chiefs" in the Pawnee culture. The Seven Brothers and the Circle of Chiefs are positioned opposite of each other in the sky and trade places with each other every twelve hours. On or around November 21, Pleiades, or the Seven Brothers, was directly overhead and shined through the smoke holes in the Pawnee observation lodges at midnight, signaling to the tribe that the longest night of the year, the Winter Solstice, was exactly one month away. The Pawnee astronomers knew and recorded that, although it was unseen in the brightness of day, the Circle of Chiefs would be directly overhead of the village at noon on November 21. It was also in late November that the Pleiades and the Circle of Chiefs shared the night sky. As the sun set, star watchers could see the Circle of Chiefs in the sky to the northwest and the Seven Brothers in the northeast sky.

The Pawnee sky watchers also observed that as each day passed, the stars would appear in the same spot in the night sky, approximately four minutes earlier. As each month passed, the stars' positions were a full two hours earlier. The Native American astronomers planned the major Pawnee celebration, the Spring Awakening, according to star placement. They tracked the movement of the "Swimming Ducks," their name for two small stars, as they swam along the "Path of Departed Souls," which we call the Milky Way. When the Swimming Ducks reached a certain point in their journey, the Pawnee people knew it was time to celebrate the impending return of spring and the awakening of the land, by preparing the soil for planting. But it was the Seven Brothers who told them when to plant. According to historical records, the Pleiades constellation would appear in the lodge's smoke hole at sunset and the Circle of Chiefs would appear at sunrise, several weeks before the vernal equinox, which occurs near March 20. The Pawnee believed this was the stars' signal to them to begin their spring planting. The stars that comprise the Seven Brothers would then be invisible to the Pawnee sky watchers for the next six months because the Earth faced them only in the daylight. When the star cluster again appeared in the smoke hole, it was near the autumnal equinox, or September 22, to inform the Pawnee that harvest time had come.

It is interesting to note what is missing from the Pawnee star charts. While most other cultures developed lunar-based calendars, made special note of the Summer Solstice, and charted the sun's movement in the sky, the Pawnees focused their attention mainly on the stars. Even though the sun and moon played roles in their myths and legends, it was the stars that were of most importance in the lives of the Pawnee tribe.

Although the Pawnee astronomers erroneously claimed the stars had fallen to Earth in a pivotal moment in the history and culture of the tribe, it was actually a meteor shower, more specifically the 1833 Leonid meteor shower that became known around the nation and in Pawnee legend as "The Year the Stars Fell." The Leonid meteor shower occurs every year in early to mid-November. This annual meteor shower originates from the constellation Leo, from which it gets its name. The 1833 Leonid meteor shower, occurring on November 13, was one of the most spectacular meteor showers on record, for a few reasons. A comet named Tempel-Tuttle circles around the sun every 32 years and six months. Even though the Earth passes through the comet's orbit every year, the comet is closest to the Earth and the Sun every 33 years, which fell in 1833. Additionally, the conditions on the night of November 13, 1833 were ideal – clear and cloudless. This meant there was a brilliant and dazzling display of shooting stars that surprised and frightened many people.

Historical accounts show that white European settlers, African slaves, and Native Americans alike all watched the meteor shower with fear and panic, most truly believing that the stars were falling to Earth and the world was ending. The Pawnee Indians, however, remained calm. One Pawnee folklore tells the story of Pahokatawa, a warrior who was slaughtered by his enemies and fed to wild animals. The gods brought him back to life and he fell back to Earth as a meteor. He told his people that meteors showering the Earth, whether it be one meteor or many, was not an omen that the world was ending. So, when the 1833 Leonid shower began and the Pawnees became fearful, the chief gently reminded his people to "remember the words of Pahokatawa." Unlike the other Native American tribes, the Pawnees experienced the 1833 Leonid shower spectacularly unafraid.

5 LANGUAGE AND PICTOGRAMS

"Mainly, these were the sounds of bird wings rising up into the sky, rustling trees, they cry of the mourning dove, and the rippling wind. They were the first nonhuman sounds I heard because my family spent most of the time outdoors. This awareness was followed by other sounds of life embracing me with deep sighs and measured breathes. Those human sounds then became syllables, or vocables, and voice patterns with intonations and inflections. Eventually and inexplicable, they turned into words such as Waconda, meaning Creator, or the Great Mystery of Life, and waduge, meaning to eat, and Mayah, the Earth. Single words became explosions of sounds and images, and these reveled outward in strings of sentences or melodies and songs."
~Anna Lee Walters, award-winning author and Pawnee member

The native tongue of the Pawnee people is a branch of the Caddoan linguistic family, a cluster of similar languages that are spoken by Native American tribes in the plains states. The word Pawnee comes from the words Panee or Pani, which mean wolf. In fact, the sign language motion for the Pawnee people involved using one's hands to make wolf ears. Like many Native America languages, it is critically endangered, however efforts are underway to preserve the language. Pawnee is one of five languages in this family, which also includes Caddo, Kitsai, Arikara, and Wichita. Of these, Kitsai has completely died out and the Wichita language only remains in audio recordings and written texts. Estimates contend that there are fewer than 25 speakers of Caddo, only five Arikara speakers, and about 20 speakers of Pawnee. The Pawnee language has two distinct dialects, the South Band and the Skiri. Starting in 2007, the Pawnee Nation has been making progress in protecting the language by introducing it in area high school language classes and by offering classes for adult learners who want to learn the language.

Currently, the North American Indian Studies Research Institute, based at Indiana University in Bloomington, Indiana, is thoroughly and painstakingly documenting the Pawnee language as part of their initiative to study and protect the endangered languages of the United States, Canada, and Mexico. The Plains Indian language project, funded by the National Endowment for the Humanities, the National Science Foundation, and the various American Indian tribal organizations, aims to study the unique linguistic elements of the Pawnee native tongue, as well as track influences on the language from outside sources, such as interactions with English and Spanish settlers and neighboring Native American tribes. Audio and video recordings of native speakers of the language are being cataloged and documented, and teaching material is being produced to help others learn the language.

There are eight consonant sounds in the Pawnee language, and four short-long vowel sound pairs. In linguistic terms, the language is polysynthetic. What this means is that the each sound has its own meaning and can be combined into long sentence-words in which each independent sound contributes to the overall meaning of the phrase.

The Pawnee tribe was one of the numerous Native American tribes to employ a form of sign language known as Plains Sign Language, or First Nation Sign Language. The Plains Sign Language served as a mode of communication between different groups and tribes who often spoke completely different languages or indiscernible dialects of the same language. By some estimates, Plains Sign Language was used by speakers of as many as 37 languages. The sign language is most likely as old as the Native American spoken language. Plains Sign Language found its way into spiritual ceremonies and storytelling as well. The earliest European explorers to encounter the Pawnee and other Plains Indians noted that the sign language was well-developed and comprehensive.

Linguists believe the Plains Sign Language existed independent of oral language; there is no direct link between a gesture and a spoken word in one of the languages. The sign language consisted of four key parts – shape of the hand, location of the hand, movement of the hand, and orientation of the hand.

A side effect of Native American assimilation into the American culture was a decline in the number of Plains Sign Language speakers. Only a few remain today.

Interestingly, the 2016 hit film "The Revenant," starred Leonardo DiCaprio as a frontiersman who was left for dead by his party. Set in the 1820s, the director, Alejandro González Iñárritu included both the Pawnee and Arikara languages in the film. Although the director's goal was historical accuracy, the inclusion of these dwindling languages served to bring attention to them and inspired more people to learn to speak these languages.

When the Pawnees assimilated into the culture of the European settlers, they adopted the Latin alphabet and applied it to their oral language. Prior to this, the Pawnees did not have a written language in the modern sense of the term. Instead they used a pictogram-based written language. Symbols, drawings, and signs depicting important events and people were drawn or painted on their clothing and tepees. Often, these pictograms told stories or legends and recounted big hunts that included images of horses, weapons, and wounded animals. Still others illustrated the importance of astronomy to the Pawnee people, with the sun, moon, stars, and constellations being shown. Most of these pictograms were not placed on permanent items like cave walls or cliff faces, therefore, many have been lost over time.

6 THE PAWNEE WAR

"He [Sky Chief] had killed a buffalo and was skinning it when the advance guard of the Sioux shot and wounded him. The Chief attempted to reach his horse, but before he was able to mount, several of the enemy surrounded him. He died fighting. A Pawnee, who was skinning a buffalo a short distance away, but managed to escape, told me how Sky Chief died. The Pawnees were putting up a splendid fight, but the odds were against them."
~John W. Williamson, of the Genoa Agency, eyewitness to the Pawnee Massacre of 1873

The Pawnees were fierce warriors and skirmishes with neighboring tribes were not uncommon as different groups of people attempted to claim the best hunting grounds. In order to look more fearsome, the Pawnee warriors tattooed their bodies and painted them with war paint. In fact, the Pawnee people believed the creator god, Tirawa, showed them how to tattoo.

Although there were occasional inter-tribal conflicts between different bands of the Pawnee Indians, most of the hostilities were between the Pawnee people and the Sioux, also known as the Lakota. One such battle occurred on August 5, 1873, and became known as the Pawnee War, or the Canyon Massacre.

Setting the stage for this battle was the first Pawnee land cession to the United States government some forty years prior. The Pawnee sold a large plot of land, located south of the Platte River in Nebraska, in 1833. The site of the Canyon Massacre of 1873 lies on this piece of land. Since the land cession, the Pawnee had entered into an agreement with the U.S. government that allowed them to retain hunting rights to their ancestral lands, which encompassed areas around the Platte and Republican rivers. The Lakota also had an arrangement with the U.S. government concerning this land. An 1868 treaty gave them permission to hunt along the Republican River. This put Pawnee and Lakota hunters in regular contact with each other, and the encounters were often violent in nature. Both groups appealed to the United States to intercede, but the conflict remained unresolved. The hostilities came to a head in 1873.

On August 4 of 1873, a hunting party of about 400 Pawnee people, including women and children, were returning home after a successful hunt when they stopped to camp in what is now Trenton, Nebraska. With the hunters, were trail agents John W. Williamson and Lester Beach Platt, representing the United States government.

Nearby, a Lakota hunting party, led by Chief Little Wound, was also hunting near the Republican River. At the Lakota hunting camp was Chief Two Strikes and Bureau of Indian Affairs agent, Stephen Eastes. When the scouts returned to the Lakota encampment, they told of a large Pawnee gathering. The Lakota had recently been steered away from fighting the Utes by government agent, Antoine Janis, and were angry and defiant. Chief Little Wound told Janis that his men did not want to sacrifice men and horses to the Pawnee again. The Lakota warriors, numbering around 1,000, prepared to attack the Pawnee before they could attack first.

They waited until the morning hours of August 5, when the Pawnees entered a canyon, pursuing their animal prey. Following close behind were the women and children. The Lakota lay in wait and attacked the hunters. Taken by surprise, the Pawnee warriors quickly formed a defensive stance and prepared for battle. Williamson tried to negotiate a peace talk but could not ride out of the pack of Pawnees without being turned back by a hail of Lakota bullets.

After the battle was over, the Pawnee survivors told tales that became legend. In one such tale, the Pawnee warrior, Sky Chief, bravely fought for much of the battle. But when it became apparent that the Lakota would be victorious, Sky Chief killed his own son in front of the enemy, shouting to them that they would not get his son.

The Pawnee women, according to legends, dumped the bundles off their horses, abandoning the meat from their recent hunt and their other provisions. They attempted to flee the canyon on the horses, but the Lakota warriors fired upon them from both sides of the canyon.

When the dust had settled, an estimated 100 to 300 Pawnee men, women, and children, including infants, were dead in the canyon. Many of the Pawnee warriors' bodies had been mutilated and desecrated. Several of the Pawnee women were found unclothed, the victims of rape before they were killed. Reports said only one Lakota warrior was killed.

While the Lakota celebrated their victory over the Pawnee, the Pawnee survivors mourned the deaths of their loved ones and nursed their battle wounds. Numerous Pawnees were taken prisoner by the Lakota, but they were released after intervention on the part of the Bureau of Indian Affairs and the United States government.

The Pawnee Massacre, as the event became known, was the largest Plains Indians skirmish and the final battle between the Pawnee and the Lakota. It was deemed the bloodiest fight between the two tribes. The United States government took notice of the event and used it to fuel their initiative to keep the Native Americans under control and confined on reservation where they could not cause trouble. In 1925, the Pawnee and the Lakota finally smoked a peace pipe at the site of the Pawnee Massacre as a symbolic gesture that the animosity between the two bands of Native Americas was over.

A monument commemorating the Pawnee Massacre was built outside of Trenton. When it was dedicated on September 26, 1930, it was the very first historical marker in Nebraska. Dubbed the Massacre Canyon Monument, it sits on a three-acre park that includes a small museum displaying Lakota and Pawnee tribal items.

7 INTERACTION WITH THE WHITE MAN

"The Great Spirit made us all – he made my skin red, and yours white; he placed us on this earth, and intended that we should live differently from each other."
~Petalesharo, Pawnee Chief (1797-1832)

Most historians believe that the first white man to encounter the Pawnee people was Francisco Vasquez de Coronado. This meeting took place in 1541. After that, there is not much textual evidence proving interactions between the Pawnee Indians and Europeans until English, French, and Spanish explorers made forays into the Great Plains in the 1600s and 1700s. It was during that time that the Native Americans were introduced to the horse. When they first saw a white man riding a horse, they believed it to be a human-beast hybrid monster. Soon, however, the horse would change the way of life for the Pawnee, as did interactions with the white man.

Frontiersmen and European settlers were attracted to fertile, treeless prairies of the Great Plains and moved into the areas that had been the traditional territory of the Pawnee for more than a thousand years. This was problematic to the expanding United States government which had designs on settling the entire continent. For the Pawnee, whose concept of land ownership greatly differed from that of the white man, having their land invaded by foreign intruders who turned the soil and disturbed the hunting grounds was seen as a threat. Raids on frontier settlements were a common response. The U.S. government viewed this aggression as a problem that needed to be solved.

The first government treaty with the Pawnee people occurred in 1818 and served as a precedent for future treaties, including the 1825 Treaty at

Fort Atkinson which stipulated that the Pawnee and several other Native American groups would only trade with citizens of the United States. In this treaty, the Native Americans were forced to acknowledge the United States as the supreme law of the land and accept the government's promise of protection. The 1833 Treaty at Grand Pawnee Village gave the lands lying south of the Platte River to the U.S. government. The Treaty at Fort Childs in 1848 ceded a 60-mile swath of land along the Platte River. In the final treaty, the 1857 Treaty at Table Creek, the Pawnee agreed to move onto a reservation located on the Platte River at the Loup Fork.

As the United States grew increasingly more dedicated to westward expansion, the traditional way of life for the Pawnee people underwent a series of changes to accommodate the outside pressures. The Pawnee grew reliant on horses for hunting and transportation. Game animals that the Pawnee hunted for food, such as deer and buffalo, became scarce and the open grasslands were turned into farm fields. Pioneers built their houses on traditional Pawnee land. Add to this the forced displacement of Native American tribes from east of the Mississippi River, who now flooded the Pawnee territory, placing more demands on the dwindling resources in the area.

Disease was a side effect of the Pawnee's interactions with the white man. A cholera outbreak in 1849 killed an estimated 1,000 Native Americans. A few years later, in 1852, a smallpox epidemic left the Pawnee villages decimated. The on-going hostilities with enemy tribes, particularly the Lakota, also reduced the Pawnee populations. The Pawnee people agreed, in 1874, to start a two-year process of relocation to a reservation further west and to hang up their weapons.

The Pawnee people supplied scouts to help the U.S. Army during the Plains Indian wars, most likely because they wanted the Army on their side after continued hostilities with the Lakota. Ninety-five Pawnee scouts served in the Powder River Exposition alongside Army soldiers, fighting against the Lakota, as well as the Cheyenne and Arapaho. Afterwards, Pawnee scouts were used to protect workers building the transcontinental railway line for the Union Pacific Railroad as it made its way through what is now Nebraska and Wyoming.

Throughout the 1800s, the United States government tried to persuade the Pawnee people to adopt a lifestyle more like the white man. It started with farming. The Pawnee were encouraged to abandon their traditional farming techniques in favor of European style farming. Next came the missionaries and a long-running and concerted effort to convert the Pawnee people to Christianity. As towns of white men sprang up across the Plains, Pawnee children were sent to pioneer schoolhouses for a white man education. The Pawnee people resisted all of this change, preferring their traditional way of life to that of the white man, but with the decline of the buffalo, the Pawnees were forced to reevaluate their situation. Many felt that acclimating to the white man ways, and living on the reservation, was the only viable option to preserve what little of their culture remained.

Forfeiting their Nebraska land, the Pawnee started the relocation process to move to a reservation in Oklahoma beginning in 1874. Unbeknownst to them, the Pawnee agent for the Bureau of Indian Affairs was working to establish a new, permanent reservation for the Pawnee people. The area he selected was south of the Osage Reservation between the Cimarron and Arkansas Rivers. Once the Pawnee leaders approved this reservation site, the four bands of the tribe each claimed a territory within the reservation as its own. The elders attempted to retain the traditional way of life with communal farm fields, and multifamily dwellings, as well as a class system within the village community. But the pull of modern ways was too strong. Within a short period of time, the once tight-knit bands who lived and worked so closely together gave way to individual houses and farms, and a population who spoke English more than their native tongue. Indian agents targeted many of the old Pawnee beliefs, such as dances and polygamy, by labeling them as immoral. The old Pawnee heritage was nearly gone.

When the Pawnee moved to the reservation, they numbered nearly 2,000. But close proximity to the white settlers meant more sickness was brought into the Pawnee community. Adequate health care was nonexistent and the living conditions were less than sanitary. As a result, the death rate among the Pawnee people rose considerably. By the turn of the century, the population dropped to slightly more than 600.

Reservation life also meant that the Pawnee people had easier access to alcohol and gambling, vices that were highly attractive, and highly addictive for the Pawnees. Two colorful characters emerged from this era; outlaw, teenage girls who illegally sold whiskey to the Pawnees. Their names were Little Britches and Cattle Annie.

Little Britches, whose given name was Jennie Stevenson, and Cattle Annie, who was born Anna Emmaline McDoulet, dressed themselves like men and smuggled alcohol into the Pawnee and Osage reservations. Experienced with rifles and excellent riders, the pair eluded capture and drifted in and out of area outlaw gangs. They even excelled at stealing horses. The duo was captured, but each only served a few months in jail at the Massachusetts Correctional Institution, which was one of the few jails in the United States that was set up to house female inmates. The girls were released to their parents. Although their crime spree barely lasted two years, the teenage outlaws and their antics became well-known through news reports that circulated across the county.

The Pawnee Industrial Boarding School was not large enough to teach all of the children of the tribe, so the BIA set up several schools away from the reservations. By 1879, most of the Pawnee youngsters were enrolled in schools in Pennsylvania, Oklahoma, Kansas, or Virginia, such as the Carlisle Indian Industrial School, the Chilocco Indian Agricultural School, the Haskell Indian Nation University, and the Hampton Institute. The majority of children who were school-aged were living off the reservation at boarding schools.

The Pawnees were unorganized and unrecognized for 30 years after the turn of the century, until the Indian Reorganization Act and the Oklahoma Indian Welfare Act, both of which were passed in the 1930s, provided Native American tribes with legal status within the U.S. government. The Pawnee re-wrote their tribal constitution in 1936 and set up a dual governing body, comprised of a chiefs' council and business council, each with eight members. It fell to the business council to negotiate with the United States government on matters that pertained to the Pawnee people. It took another 30 years of discussions and negotiations before the Pawnee were able to lawfully take back ownership of tribal lands, located near the present-day town of Pawnee. In 1968, the tribe acquired the land and converted a cluster of abandoned buildings, that once housed the Pawnee Indian School, into a tribal center.

The subject of U.S. citizenship was complex for Native Americans, including the Pawnee. The 14th Amendment stated in 1868 that all people who were born in the United States were citizens, including naturalized citizens. Native Americans, however, were excluded in this amendment. The subject was revisited again in 1870 when a Senate Judiciary committee clarified the wording of the 14th Amendment, writing "the 14th Amendment to the Constitution has no effect whatever upon the status of the Indian tribes." This didn't stop some Pawnee from seeking citizenship. There were other pathways to citizenship for Native Americans. One could, for example, marry a white person or join the United States military.

In 1924, the government passed the Snyder Act, commonly called Indian Citizenship Act, which was signed into law by President Calvin Coolidge. This act bestowed full U.S. citizenship to all Native Americans. The act was drawn up by Homer P. Snyder of New York and allowed the thousands of Native Americas who fought during the first World War, in all branches of the military, to receive the military benefits that were offered to all other veterans. Executing the Indian Citizenship Act added between 125,000 and 300,000 new citizens to the country. Even with their newly-acquired citizenship, not all Native Americans were granted voting rights. Through the 1930s, there were seven states that refused to recognize Native American citizenship. By 1947, only two hold-outs remained, New Mexico and Arizona. Both states were court-ordered to recognize the voting rights of indigenous people.

Today, the Pawnee Nation, as it is now called, is enjoying a resurgence of interest in their Native American culture and history, while laying a foundation for future growth and success. In regularly held social and heritage celebrations, traditional Pawnee singing and dancing is showcased. Traditional garb and spiritual rituals are also a part of these festivities, which have evolved from the Ghost Dances of a century ago. The Pawnee reservation has become a hub for the Pawnees. They have numerous municipal services, including police and fire departments, a tribal court, health care facilities, a library, a senior center, administrative offices, a fitness center, and an educational center.

Pawnees have made their impact on the world around them as well. Kevin Gover serves as the director of the National Museum of the American Indian in Washington, D.C. Moses "Chief" Yellow Horse was a pitcher for the Pittsburg Pirates in 1921 and 1922. Anna Lee Walters is a poet, teacher, and the author of the 1988 novel, *Ghost Singer*. And members of the EchoHawk family have been active in politics. Larry EchoHawk, a lawyer, was the director of the Bureau of Indian Affairs and served as the Attorney General of Idaho from 1991 to 1995. Most recently, in 2012, he was named the General Authority of The Church of Jesus Christ of Latter-day Saints. His brother, John EchoHawk, also a lawyer, founded the Native American Rights Fund and served as the director of the Bureau of Indian Affairs during the presidency of Barack Obama. John and Larry's cousin, Walter EchoHawk is a lawyer in Oklahoma and the staff attorney for the NaviAmerican Rights Fund, which represents Native American groups and individuals in legal matters. He was also a key figure in the Native American Graves Protection and Reparation Act. An author as well as a lawyer, he penned several books including *The Courts of the Conqueror: The Ten Worst Indian Law Cases Ever Decided* and *Battlefields and Burial Grounds*.

Fierce. Proud. Determined. These are words used to describe the Pawnee people when the European settlers first encountered them centuries ago. Much has changed for the Pawnees since then, yet these three words can still be used to describe their character and demeanor.

Made in United States
Orlando, FL
28 March 2022

10201428R00021